Lily Lynn
and the
Victory Dance

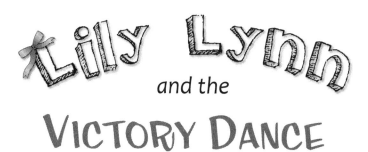

Lily Lynn

and the

Victory Dance

KELSEY MAXELL

ILLUSTRATED BY AMANDA GEORGE

Omaha, Nebraska

©2015 Kelsey Maxell

All rights reserved. No part of this book may be used or reproduced by any means, graphic, electronic, or mechanical, including photocopying, recording, taping or by any information storage retrieval system without the express written permission of the publisher, except in the case of brief quotations embodied in critical articles and reviews.

For information, address the publisher:
Building Champions Publishing
c/o Concierge Marketing Inc.
13518 L. Street
Omaha, NE 68137

Paperback ISBN : 978-0-9963465-1-1
Mobi ISBN: 978-0-9963465-2-8
EPUB: ISBN: 978-0-9963465-3-5
LCCN: 2015939532

Library of Congress Data on file with the publisher

Printed in the United States of America.

10 9 8 7 6 5 4 3 2

To Lilia and Addyson–
I hope your life is full
of Victory Dances

CHAPTER 1

The second hand on the clock crawled at a snail's pace and the minutes were frozen.

Tick.

Tick.

Tick.

Time stood still and I thought I was going to die of boredom. My teacher, Mrs. George, was rambling again about the importance of writing with word choice. Here is a sentence with some word choices for you, Mrs. George: "I am hungry and ready for recess. Oh wait, I mean; I am famished and prepared for extra-curricular play."

My full name is Lilia Lynn, but I go by Lily. Apparently, the day I was born I was sweet and delicate like a flower and my mom and dad thought the name was a perfect fit. Now that I have grown into a competitive sports freak, I am sure that they are rethinking the sweet and delicate name idea. At least they didn't name me Tulip or Chrysanthemum.

My older brother Owen is thirteen. He isn't always so thrilled to have a tag-along sister, but he tolerates me pretty well. Our family lives in a peachy colored two-story house in Lincoln, Nebraska. Our neighborhood is great because if the temperature is above thirty degrees, kids are outside playing until dark. All of the neighborhood kids are boys, except me. I really had no choice—either I play dumb dress up and dolls alone, or I join the boys and kick butt in sports.

Mrs. George was still talking, and all I heard was "Blah, blah, blah." My mind just couldn't focus on school anymore. I stared out the window and saw that the fifth graders were on the football field executing masterful plays. I watched as a Hail

Mary pass was thrown, tipped, and then caught by the offense for a touchdown. Without thinking, I jumped up as if I were in the action and screamed out, "Touchdown, Baby!"

Immediately, I covered my mouth and realized what I had just done. My entire third grade class, including my teacher, Mrs. George, was staring at me. My classmates let out a few giggles, but Mrs. George's face was a bit more strained. Her dark bushy eyebrows scrunched close together and her lips were tightly pursed. It definitely was a face of disappointment. I was busted.

Mrs. George tucked her spiraled jet-black hair behind her ears and huffed, "Thank you for your enthusiasm Lily. We know you love sports, but right now you are in class and you need to pay attention. Anyway, sports are for boys, and you, my dear, are a lady and you should act like one."

There it was again. I imagine this is what it feels like to be hit by a ninety-mile-an-hour fastball. It wasn't that my teacher called me out in front of

the entire class or that my classmates were giggling at my somewhat embarrassing and spastic shout out. I could handle the embarrassment. Her words got me right in the gut. They were the same words that I had heard over and over again by too many people, "Sports are for boys. Sports are for boys. Sports are for boys."

Following Mrs. George's comment about my poor choices in life, it was finally time for lunch.

The best thing about my elementary school was the kids. The kids seem to be the only ones that totally understand me and accept my love for sports. The two greatest kids of all are my best friends Carter and Carly. Carter and Carly are twins, and the three of us are inseparable. Carly is great to talk to about clothes and boy bands, and Carter is great because he loves sports too.

I have always eaten lunch with the girls. And after lunch they have always understood that I probably am not going to swing on the tire swing, jump rope, or gossip. Instead, they just know that during recess I am always going to play wide receiver, point guard, or striker with the boys, depending what sport we play.

Today I carried my lunch tray filled with grilled chicken nuggets and green beans to a large circular table surrounded by my friends. Hot lunch is very different this year for some reason. It's supposed to be healthy. Hardly any kids bought hot lunch because the food was gross. Heaven forbid we put a touch of salt or butter on our food! I agree with the idea of healthy eating, but a little salt, butter, or sugar is okay for a girl as active me.

My friends smiled at me without a pause in the chatter or a miss in the beat. I sat down, and dove right into the conversations we left hanging from yesterday.

"So what about Olivia's birthday party? Are we all sleeping over?"

I was glad that the excitement of Olivia's party trumped my spastic "blurt out" in class earlier.

"I'm not going to be the first one to fall asleep. I think we should try to stay up all night," said Lexi.

"Yeah!" squealed Mei.

"I think we should call all the boys in the class," said Reese.

Everyone laughed and Isabella said, "Ooooo, we should call Austin and just sit on the line while he says, 'Hello, Hello, Hello' a million times!"

Jayla chimed in, "My sister told me all about a game called Truth or Dare. I think we should definitely play that! I'll ask her how to play."

"Yeah," I said, "And maybe we could toss around the football in the morning!" Everyone just stopped talking and looked at me for what seemed like ten minutes. I just smiled and crossed my eyes at them.

I ate my lunch as quickly as I could and said goodbye to the girls. It was time to get my game on. I raced out of the lunchroom and pushed open the large steel doors that led to the outdoors. The sun was shining and I had passed through the gates and entered my heaven: the playground. I reached deep into the pockets of my jacket and pulled out my batting gloves. I used these gloves not only for batting practice in baseball, but also as my receiving gloves in football. I rolled up my hot pink leggings and was ready to play. Yes, I wear hot pink leggings. I also wear large bows in my blonde hair and like to look nice. Just because I like sports doesn't mean I don't like to look pretty. Pretty girls can like sports, too.

The first two kids out on the football field are the two captains, Grayson and Malik, and they pick their teams for the day. I am never the first pick, probably because I am a girl; but I am also never the last pick, probably because I'm a great player. We only have about fifteen minutes for recess and by the time we have picked teams, there are only about ten minutes to play.

Our team was down by two because of a safety, and I knew there wasn't much time left. I needed to make something happen. At the line I looked right into Scotty's blue eyes as I planned my strategy to beat him down the field. We were head to head in our three-point stances and I gave him a smirk. Malik hiked the ball, I did a quick juke to the left and then ran to the right, leaving Scotty in the dust. Our quarterback, Benjamin M. who had the strongest arm in our grade, launched the ball in a tight spiral in my direction. I looked over my right shoulder and was positioned perfectly to snag the ball out of the air. I tucked the ball securely and sprinted the final twenty yards without getting touched, right over the goal line. I spiked the ball on the ground and did my victory dance:

Drumroll to the left

Drumroll to the right

Fist pump and a jump—Yes!

Fist pump and a jump—Yes!

Fist pump and a jump—Yes!

I'm sure my smile was as wide as an offensive lineman's booty!

The boys on my team rushed the end zone and celebrated.

"You rock Lily! You're our secret weapon," said Benjamin M.

"Faster than most, and better looking," I said while high-fiving every member of my team one by one.

Scotty wasn't thrilled. His team wasn't either. They shook their heads and put their hands over their faces while they groaned.

"Scotty, you got schooled by a giiiirrrllll," said Grayson, "Just like yesterday." The team headed for the school's doors even before the bell rang to end recess.

My day had turned from bad to really good. All because of sports.

CHAPTER 2

The afternoon went smoothly, with no major upsets, surprises or embarrassing outbursts. I tried my best not to sports-daydream out the window. Five minutes before the bell sounded, Mrs. George made a big announcement about a class project that we would be working on.

"Class, for the next few weeks, we are going to research and write a biography about a famous person from United States history."

Ugh I thought, hopefully to myself this time.

Mrs. George continued.

"Once your biographies are finalized, you will get to dress up like your character and be a part of a wax museum." As usual, she continued more, "A wax museum is where you stand frozen dressed up as your historical character. I'll snap my fingers at you, and you will instantly awaken and give your verbal report about your famous person. Then you freeze again until the next person comes along and snaps at you."

Hmmm, that actually sounds pretty cool. Man, Mrs. George was good. She just tricked an entire class, including me, to do research, write a biography, and create a presentation without one single groan. She was enthusiastic about the project and our classroom was buzzing with excitement. Mrs. George must love teaching as much as I love sports.

Brrrring!

The bell rang at 3:06 and the weekend had finally arrived. I couldn't wait until Olivia's birthday party. I sprinted home from school and began packing my overnight bag. Just as I stuffed my pajamas into my pillowcase, my mom knocked and entered my room. I'm not sure why she even knocks because she is already halfway into my room mid-knock. I guess she doesn't see the large poster sign on my door that says, *Knock before entering*. It doesn't say, *Knock and enter simultaneously*.

"Lily, we need to chat. I see that you have been busy packing, but remember you have two soccer games in the morning. The first at 8:00 and the next one at 9:00. I do not think it is the best idea for you to sleep over at the birthday party."

"Whaaaaaaaaat?" I replied with a rather snarky tone.

"Lily, calm down. You know that you can be a bear without the right amount of sleep. Your dad and I think it is best that we pick you up this evening before the other girls put their pajamas on."

"Are you kidding me, Mom? The whole point of a sleepover birthday party is that kids actually get to *sleep over*. I will be the only girl who has to leave." I could hear the tone of my voice getting higher and higher and louder and louder. "You

and Dad just want me to be miserable and have no friends. THAT'S NOT FAIR!"

I knew I had gone too far. I know speaking to my parents in that manner is unacceptable, and even worse, my mom and dad despised the words, "That's not fair." Every time those three words escape my mouth, their eyeballs get crazy big, their teeth clench, and they both look like rabid Chihuahuas. *Probably not the right time to tell her my thoughts about her amazing resemblance to a dog.*

"Lilia Lynn, it is your choice to play on a girls' soccer team and a boys' soccer team. You love these sports and if I am going to spend my weekends carting you around to your activities, you will be well-rested and will not be staying up until the wee hours of the morning at a sleepover. This is not a matter of discussion anymore, and if I hear any more attitude you will be missing the entire party and your games!"

I knew Mom meant business and even though I was still upset about the sleepover, I conceded. I refuse to lose both the party *and* my games.

I muttered, "Yes ma'am." (I know she hates to be called ma'am.)

Later that evening, when I arrived at the party the girls were painting nails and getting ready to eat pizza. I painted my nails Royal Blue, of course, to match my favorite baseball team, the Kansas City Royals. We had a pizza-eating contest and all my friends were impressed with my pizza-eating skills. They chanted "Lily, Lily, Lily," like 90,000 people were cheering me on at the World Cup in Brazil. I hammered down eight slices like a champ. It doesn't have to just be sports, any sort of competition gets me excited. I love to win.

Next, we played the best game ever invented, *Truth or Dare*. I picked Dare, but just as the girls were creating a devilish Dare the doorbell rang. It was my mom, ready to pick me up. With only seconds left to play, the girls switched my Dare to a Truth and asked me the question I knew was coming:

"Lily, who do you think is C U T E?" Jayla spelled.

Lexi and Reese both Ooooooooooo-ed (is that even a word?)

Of course in my mind I was thinking my famous words; *that's not fair*! I didn't want to answer because I knew on Monday morning everyone at school would know my secret crush. A group full of girls is the worst place to unveil any juicy information. My secret would be all over the city, state, country, world and universe in no time. The pressure was building. My face was flushed and the girls were all wide-eyed and smiling because they had caught me in a predicament. I was out of time and had to spill the Truth.

As I ran up the basement stairs to go home I hollered down at my friends, "Benjamin M.!" I could hear the *Oo La Las* and giggling as I exited Olivia's birthday party, horrified.

That night I laid in bed and struggled to get comfortable enough to fall asleep. All I could think about was the embarrassment coming Monday morning at school when everyone knew my quarterback was my secret crush.

CHAPTER 3

Dad woke me up very early Saturday morning with his famous eggs that he called *Soccer Scramble*. Even though the eggs, and the name, were rather cheesy, I went along with it because it was tradition and it made Dad smile. I gobbled the eggs up, and Dad and I began to talk about our deal of the day. Every Soccer Saturday we played a fun little game. For each goal I scored in my game I got to pick out one menu item from Burger Magic for lunch. Each game this season so far I enjoyed nuggets, fries, and a drink. Yep, that is three goals in one game. One game I even scored four goals, so I got to add a chocolate shake.

My first game was with my all-boys team, the Lincoln Lightning. As we warmed up, I could hear a few of the boys on the other team snickering about my long ponytail and that I was a girl playing with all boys.

"This should be a cakewalk; there's a girl on their team!" This behavior from the opposing boys' teams was becoming more common as I got older and it really wasn't sitting that well with me. My stomach lurched and I knew it was going to be hard to be aggressive during the game. For the first time, I wasn't confident and I felt negative thoughts seeping into my brain about where I belonged.

During the game I played left halfback. I always play on the left side because I am left footed. I just happen to have a very strong left foot and can cross the ball to the middle of the field for my teammates to score. I love how it feels to get the ball to half field, make a move around an opposing player, and use my speed to dribble down the line. Then with my strong and accurate left foot, I power the ball into the air right in front of the goal and watch my teammates head the ball or kick it into the goal. I really love to score, but assists are pretty awesome, too.

I had so many chances during the game to make a move around players and cross the ball, but I couldn't get anything going. Every time I touched the ball, the opposing team challenged me and stole the ball right from my feet. My negative thoughts were overpowering me. It was like I was frozen out on the field just watching the game that I was supposed to be playing.

Our team lost three to one.

The boys on the other team had really gotten to me before the game. I don't want to be a boy. I am not weird. I just want to play. I was mad at myself for letting their words affect me like that. I should have just showed them my awesome skills and kicked their butts in the process.

As we got into the car to race to my next game, I sat quietly and looked out the window at the lines painted on the pavement.

Mom asked, "Are you okay kiddo?" Mom is the best about understanding how I feel. "You always wear your heart on your sleeve, you know."

I have no idea what that means, but what I do know is she is great to talk to in these situations. My eyes began to well up with tears. I looked up at the sunroof in the car, holding the tears in place and telling myself not to blink. One blink and it would be all over. One blink and the tears would stream down my cheeks. My eyes kept filling until I couldn't take it anymore. I blinked and began to cry. I couldn't get out the words to explain myself because I was so upset. After calming down, I said, "Mom, I heard the boys on the other team say mean things about me. It made me mad and sad and frustrated. I let them get to me and I played terrible."

Mom listened and let me get it all out. The only thing she could say was, "I was afraid that eventually this would happen to you, sweetheart." We pulled into the gravel parking lot at the soccer fields and I wiped away my tears. Mom said, "It's time to refocus and get ready for your next match. I know you can do it, Lily!"

My all-girls team, the Crush—was already warming up. I ran onto the field leaving my negative thoughts behind and was ready to shine. I just needed three goals to get the meal deal and with a fourth I would have a chocolate shake. Hey, maybe even a fifth and Dad would make his all-star pancakes on Sunday morning for breakfast. After my performance during my Lightning game, I had a lot of steam to blow off and was ready to tear it up!

Following warm-ups I was feeling great…until my coach pulled me aside. "Lily, I wanted to let you know that for this game you are going to play defense." My mouth dropped open and it felt like a volleyball had been pounded right into my throat. I couldn't talk. I was in total shock.

My coach continued, "I need to give the other girls on the team an opportunity to play striker and score goals. Also, this will give you a chance to improve your defensive skills and work on your goal kicks. Everyone on the team should know how to play all of the positions on the field."

This Soccer Saturday stinks. How can I shine playing fullback practicing my defensive skills when I should be striker scoring goals and doing my victory dance?

I played defense for the entire forty minutes. I did not smile once and my bad attitude was showing. I felt lazy and my competitive edge had disappeared. I let girls make moves on me and blow by me. I didn't even care. *If they were going to make me play defense, then I would give them the worst defense they had ever seen*, I thought to myself. My heart knew this wasn't right, but I couldn't stop myself, and I continued to act completely ridiculous for the entire game. Boy, was I going to hear it from my parents. My attitude was not respectful and I definitely was not being a team player, but I couldn't help it.

Following the game, I had no idea if we won or lost, and I really didn't care. I shook hands with the other team and pouted all the way to the car. During the car ride home I realized that I hadn't scored a goal all day long. For the first time, I wouldn't get a meal deal, a single treat, or a measly packet of ketchup.

The only thing I got was a huge lecture about being a team player and sent to my room for the rest of the day.

"Lily, those other girls play defense for you every single game so you can score goals. Today was your turn to let someone else feel what it is like to kick the ball into the net. I'm disappointed in the way you acted. I'm half tempted to have you call your coach and your entire team to apologize for not being a team player."

I gasped. I couldn't imagine the embarrassment of calling all the girls. What would I say? 'I'm sorry, I'm a bad teammate? I'm sorry, I'm a bad friend? Will you ever forgive me? Will you still play defense for me when I'm on offense again?' Ugh. I silently pleaded with the universe that my parents would not make me do that. Then I promised the universe that if I had to play defense again, I would give my best effort.

The rest of the weekend continued to stink, I spent most of my time in my room grounded, which was probably pretty good considering my luck lately. Mom gave me a long list of chores to keep me busy in my room. I sorted and matched my socks, reorganized the clothes in my closet, cleaned out my junk drawer in my desk, and of course I could not have music or electronics to keep me company. After finally completing the last chore on mom's seven foot long list, I ate dinner and then had to do the dishes with Owen.

I climbed into bed exhausted and was asleep within seconds.

I was glad for the weekend to be over. Monday morning I sprang out of bed before my soccer alarm clock even buzzed, which was rather unusual for a morning grumpy bear like myself. The weekend was behind me, my room was spotless, and I was ready to start a new week out fresh. I was feeling pumped up again.

And then it dawned on me. I was so focused on my soccer disasters from the weekend that I forgot all about the birthday party at Olivia's and the horror of unveiling my secret crush!

And so my bad luck continued.

CHAPTER 4

"I'm sick," I groaned. Mom didn't buy it. "Get up and get dressed. You'll feel better once you get moving." I tried harder. I pinched my cheeks and nose until they were bright pink, and rolled and

moaned. Mom didn't buy that either. My sports skills were advanced, but I was lacking as an actress. I was overly dramatic and exaggerated and it was not an award-winning performance.

I got dressed and headed to the door. Mom forced my backpack on my back, checked my forehead and said "No fever, honey! You're so lucky!" she said in her overly happy, high-pitched voice. "You don't want to be late for school." She gave me a quick kiss on the cheek, and I drudgingly walked to school.

I hid behind the pine trees that lined the playground where no one could see me until the first bell rang and I was forced to face all of my classmates who undoubtedly knew my big secret. By this time I am sure aliens on undiscovered planets were gabbing about my love life. I kept my head down and zipped toward the coat hall. I slinked through the mob of kids, hung my backpack on the hook and made myself invisible as I walked into my classroom.

I slid into my seat and slumped low without acknowledging any of the "Hi Lily!" greetings I heard. I attempted to camouflage myself with my desk. I made no eye contact with anyone except for Mrs. George. She was probably the only one who didn't know my secret. Unless it was a fascinating discussion about the six writing traits or long division, Mrs. George was the only one out of the loop about hot gossip. I was thankful for her today, and she seemed surprised and thankful that I wasn't gazing out the window to daydream. Little did she know that I was not thinking about her reading fluency lesson, and was only trying to save face in front of my friends.

The more I stared at Mrs. George, the more no one could look at me and make a heart shape with their hands, make a kissy face, or bat their eyes at me with an *Oo La La*-face mocking my newly unveiled crush on Benjamin M.

We worked on equivalent fractions in math first and then completed a multiplication time test.

I'm one of the fastest in the class and even beat the math genius, Grayson, most of the time. My motto is: Fast in school, fast on the field.

After math, we did a science experiment working independently with magnetism and electricity. We each had a magnet and we had to see if the magnet attracts or repels the different materials. Magnets are a lot like people.

Finally, we finished our morning with another exciting writing lesson about "voice." All I could think about was how I wished my voice hadn't worked last Friday night during Truth or Dare.

This was the only time in my life that the morning flew by and it was already time for lunch. I couldn't face anyone, so I walked up to Mrs. George and asked her if I could use the restroom. She nodded her head and said, "Yes, when you're finished, meet the rest of the class at lunch."

Phew! This bought me a few more minutes of alone time.

I went into the bathroom and locked myself into the last stall. I sat with my legs crossed on the toilet seat so my feet didn't show under the door, and began some intense brainstorming to come up with a plan to avoid seeing my classmates. My face was starting to heat up and turn red just thinking about the embarrassment to come.

Suddenly I realized that the bathroom I was using was completely unoccupied except for me, of course. The entire third grade was at lunch and recess and the teachers were in the lounge eating their lunches. I was safe and sound right there in the bathroom and no one would be here until lunch and recess were over.

Brilliant plan.

In what seemed like an eternity, I heard the footsteps of the third graders tromping in from lunch and recess. I slipped out of the bathroom and into the mob of kids without anyone noticing my absence. It was perfect! For the rest of my life, until I graduated from high school, I would spend lunch and recess in the bathroom and never face my friends again.

And then my stomach growled angrily and I realized my plan was a flop—unless I wanted to starve to death.

During the afternoon I continued to glue my stare at my teacher, and when the bell rang I ran home like a track star never looking back once at my school and my friends.

At dinner that night, Mom made her typical yellow meal. Everything always seemed to be yellowish. Chicken with yellow gravy, sweet corn, and pineapple. I was starving because I hadn't eaten since breakfast and wolfed down my food. Mom grinned from ear to ear thinking she was Rachael Ray, the cooking lady, and that she had just made an All-Star dish on the Food Channel.

I was pretty quiet at the dinner table and thankful I didn't have a practice that night. I excused myself from the table, took a shower, and told my parents I had to work on homework for the rest of the night. It was getting pretty lonely avoiding both my friends and my family, but I just wanted to be alone—and a discussion with my parents about revealing my crush to everyone at the party would be too weird.

The next day I packed a snack in a zipped baggie, and asked Mrs. George right before recess to use the restroom again. I ate my snack in the restroom and thought my plan of avoiding my friends would work out perfectly. I WAS WRONG!

That afternoon, after locking myself into my delightful commode-cottage, taking a seat on my super-comfy porcelain throne, and munching on my decadent meal of stale pretzel twists, (Mrs. George would be proud of my word choice.) I heard the bathroom door swing open, footsteps, and a knock on the door of my stall.

I WAS CAUGHT.

Mrs. George said politely, "Lily, finish up in there and meet me in the classroom." *Busted*. Then I heard her footsteps going away from me and felt the air from the door as she opened it quickly and left. I flushed the toilet pretending that I had actually used the restroom, washed my hands, and exited the bathroom. I was shaking with nerves and was surprised to see more than Mrs. George in the classroom. My best friends, Carter and Carly, were also waiting for me.

My elementary school is great because the kids like me and I like them. Well I guess that can also be a major downer because when they like you they also notice when you disappear for lunch and recess.

Apparently Carly told Carter that I hadn't been to the lunch table today and Carter told Carly that I was missing from football at recess, too. He probably noticed because they can't win without their best wide receiver. They decided to tell Mrs. George and the three of them played detective and cased out my hideout.

I had to come clean. "I'm sorry guys. When I left Olivia's party the other day when we were playing Truth or Dare, I blurted out who I like. Truth is, I didn't want anyone to know that."

Carly and Carter laughed. Carly said, "Your secret crush news was *sooo last week*!"

Carter added, "Jake forgot to change out of his superhero pajama pants this morning and wore them to school under his jeans. That's what everyone is talking about today."

Carly reminded me, "You're tough, Lily, and even if someone did make fun of you, you can handle it because you're stronger than all of the girls and most of the boys!" We all laughed and I felt better.

Then Mrs. George spoke in her soft, but strong voice, "Being a stowaway in the bathroom wasn't your best idea, and sometimes being embarrassed is just part of life. Remember last week when I had toilet paper stuck to my shoe? That was embarrassing for me, but you just have to learn to laugh at yourself sometimes."

Maybe Mrs. George wasn't so bad after all. I promised myself to really try to listen to her lessons from now on, even the lessons that were right before lunch and recess.

Carly, Carter, and Mrs. George were right. I faced my fears and decided to join the living. It was pretty easy because I had such good friends, and before I knew it everything was back to normal… until later that afternoon when Benjamin M. and I were partners for a Reader's Theater and he flashed his perfectly-dimpled smile my way proving Mrs. George's hypothesis about magnetism.

CHAPTER 5

As the school days progressed, the talk around school fortunately never drifted to my love life—it was about something even crazier; SCHOOL. The whole school was buzzing about Mrs. George's wax museum biography project. In just a few short weeks I was going to be presenting to the entire school. Everyone was busy researching, creating their costumes and props, and preparing their speeches. I was doing a great job acting like I was busy in the classroom and at home. I told everyone in my class that my biography was going to be a surprise. It *was* a surprise...even to me.

I am extremely competitive in sports, pizza eating, math, and now even in history. In fact, I wanted my history project to be HISTORICAL. My biography presentation would be the grand slam of all projects, one for the record books. Later in life they would call me back to Zeman Elementary School and I would be inducted into the Zeman Elementary Hall of Fame for my stupendous and brilliant biography project.

In the midst of my Hall of Fame daydream, Mrs. George called me up to her desk. Everyone was busy on the computers finding tons of facts on their famous person. I was on my computer too—but I was checking out the division standings on the Major League Baseball website. I clicked out of that website so nobody would snoop, and bounced up to Mrs. George's desk with a smile. "Yes, Mrs. George?"

Mrs. George rose slowly from her chair and put a hand on her hip. She wasn't smiling. In a falsely friendly tone, she asked,"So… how is your project coming along, Lily?"

"Great!" I quickly replied with a lie and hustled back to my desk. I made it to my seat, opened my laptop back up, and again put on a great show of fake working.

A moment later Mrs. George politely asked me to return to her desk. This time I bounced a lot less and drug my feet a whole lot more towards her desk…the desk of doom.

Mrs. George looked at me over her glasses—or should I say she looked *through* me. "Who are you researching, Lily? I have list of everyone's biography, and yet I don't seem to have yours." There was nothing to say. My mouth gaped open, and no words came out. I was so busted. My eyes welled up, and I looked up towards the fluorescent-lighted ceiling, praying that my tears wouldn't escape and stream down my face.

Finally, my words formulated as my tears released onto my cheeks and the large salty droplets landed onto a pile of papers on Mrs. George's desk. "Mrs. George, I want my project

to be the best, but I can't seem to think of anyone in history to research that someone else isn't already doing."

Mrs. George stood up and said in a low whispered voice, "I remind you that our projects are due in less than two weeks. Unfortunately, Lily, I have to call your parents and let them know that you need to get moving." I could see that she was disappointed in me again, and I could hear it too. She continued, "I am very worried that you aren't going to have enough time to finish. This is a very big project and your grade for the quarter depends on it."

"Yes, Mrs. George." I muttered, and I turned and walked to my desk to stare at the computer for a little while more. I wasn't even acting like I was working this time; I was just staring at the screen wondering, *What the heck am I going to do now?*

My Hall of Fame dreams were quickly turning into the Hall of Shame.

That night, my parents were not too thrilled that Mrs. George called home. "Lily, I don't know what's gotten into you. I thought you were excited about this project," Dad said.

Mom wasn't as calm. "Lily Lynn," she began, "I don't know how in the heck you are going to get this project done if you don't even know what it is. You cannot be done with research and start writing and creating your project if you don't even know who you are researching." I thought she was done, but she was just getting started. "Lily, I am disappointed in you. Just pick someone and get moving now—and when I say now, I mean right now. You are grounded to your room until you come up with an idea for your project. Once you decide who to research, you are grounded to your room until you get caught up with the rest of the class."

Wonderful, that means I am grounded with a computer and a massive pile of books to finish my project. Fun.

I paced my room back and forth, back and forth, back and forth. I sat on my bed on one side of my room, then I leaned on the window on the other side. I laid on my bed and tried to see who I could see in the designs on my ceiling. I jumped up and down and even stood on my head to get blood to my brain. I pushed on my temples trying to squeeze some sort of idea into my head. The problem that I faced now was that all the great famous people had already been taken. Carly had Amelia Earhart, the first woman pilot to fly solo across the Atlantic Ocean. Carter had Abraham Lincoln, a great American President who helped to end slavery. Scotty had picked Neil Armstrong, the first astronaut to walk on the moon. The list went on and on.

Not only did I want to wow the entire school with my famous historical person, but also, I wanted to pick a famous person that was special to me. Someone that I would want to thank because what they did in the past changed my life for the better.

But who?

It was Thursday—family movie night—and being grounded included missing that. I knew that Owen and my parents were settling in to our make believe movie theater chairs, while I was stuck in my room. I could smell the buttery microwave popcorn. I could hear the sounds of a great movie just about to begin.

Sure enough, my family didn't just pick a great movie, they were watching *A League of Their Own*. Not only was it my favorite movie just as a movie, but it was all about a women's baseball team that was formed during World War II. Many men were fighting the war, and women got an opportunity to play professional baseball. The women traveled from town to town playing baseball and the crowds gathered to watch them play. There were strikeouts, slides into bases, double plays, and homeruns. We had watched this movie a lot, and I always dreamed that if I had lived in those days I could have played for the Rockford Peaches.

My disappointment and fear had turned to frustration earlier, and now was turning into anger. I knew that I was in trouble for not having done much of anything for a few weeks on my project, but watching my favorite movie was just downright dirty and unfair. I clenched my fists and let out a huge stream of mumbled nonsense. "AHHHHHHHH! I hate my life, I hate school, I hate my bedroom, I hate this project. I wish I was a baseball player back in the 1940s. I wish I could…."

I stopped dead in my tracks and also heard the movie pause downstairs. There was complete silence in the house. Perhaps they stopped because of my crazy wail of a scream. But in the sudden silence, I realized I had stopped because the big old light bulb was shining brightly above my head. The fog had cleared in my brain and the world made so much sense again. I finally had the perfect idea for my project!

I swung my bedroom door open and sprinted down the hallway. I flew down the stairs so fast that I tripped at the top of the staircase and tumbled down all twelve landing sharply on my arm. The pain was unbearable. My arm was throbbing as I laid there wincing in agony. Even playing sports and being hit with a volleyball in the face, or hitting my shins on benches, or scraping my knee as I slid into home, I had never in my life felt anything like this. The pain was so incredibly great and awful that the last thing I remembered was lying at the bottom of the stairs as everything grew darker and darker.

CHAPTER 6

When I awoke, I was confused by my surroundings. Thankfully I saw my mom next to me in the back seat of the car. I reached up to rub my eyes and felt an excruciating bolt of pain, and suddenly, everything went dark again.

Next, I woke up in a room that was very clean and white. It looked nothing like my bedroom at home. Then it all came back to me. My flash of brilliance in my bedroom, the idea I wanted to share with my family, and THE FALL. I looked at my arm and then at my mom again. She gave me a half-smile and I looked back at my arm.

Nurses and doctors swirled in and out of the room, poking and prodding, taking pictures, and talking in soft tones to my mom. The doctor put his hand on my shoulder and looked at me. He said, "Well, you broke your arm pretty good this time. So, Lily, what's your favorite color?" I didn't know what in the heck that had to do with anything, so of course I said, "Kansas City Royals blue."

Before long, I was sporting a lovely Kansas City Royals blue cast. *Lovely*. I slide into bases and I get kicked in the shins in soccer; I am an athlete. Athletes aren't supposed to trip on the stairs and break their arms.

When I arrived home, I got settled and went to bed. I wasn't going to school the next day, that was for sure. Given the Thursday I had had, staying home sounded pretty good.

The next day after school, I was blessed with some visitors who had heard about my accident. Carly and Carter had brought balloons, and my grandparents brought me a new book. Later on in the afternoon I heard the doorbell ring and mom answered the door. I heard talking as mom and the guest shut the door and came into the house. I was shocked by my surprise visitor as she entered the living room. It was Mrs. George!

I couldn't believe my eyes. First of all, do teachers ever leave the school? Secondly, it was kind of weird seeing Mrs. George not sporting black pants, high heels, and a blouse. She was wearing gym shorts, a t-shirt, and tennis shoes. It isn't everyday that a teacher rings your doorbell, so as you can imagine I didn't know what to say.

The first words that came to my mouth were, "What are *you* doing here?" My eyes became wide and I slapped my hand over my big mouth. I was just extremely rude to my teacher. I quickly collected my thoughts and tried again.

"I mean, Mrs. George, it is nice to see you, please come in." Mrs. George gave me a smile and sat down. Mom sat next to me, and Dad sat in his favorite chair. Mrs. George said, "Lily, how are you doing? I heard you broke your arm yesterday. Nice cast—Kansas City Royals, I presume?" It made me feel so special that a teacher would drive all the way to my house to make sure I was okay. I told her the whole story about my grand idea for my wax museum project and how I raced down the stairs and tripped.

Mrs. George stood up and patted my hair. She handed me an envelope, and said, "Lily, I hope you feel better quickly and are back at school soon. We missed you today."

I said, "Thank you, Mrs. George. For visiting me and all." After she walked out the door, I opened the envelope that she had given me. Inside was a get well card with a photograph. The card read; *Lily the ball is in your court. Sports are for girls, too.*

I looked closely at the photograph. It was a picture of a volleyball team. The photograph was worn and kind of old, but clear enough that I could read the jerseys on the players' uniforms. *Hawkeyes.* I scanned the group of girls in the photo and found an arrow pointing down with the word "Me" written over one of the girls. There, staring back at me, was a familiar face. Jet-black hair, thick eyebrows; it was a young Mrs. George! All this time she pushed me to study harder and pay attention, Mrs. George was a collegiate athlete. Mrs. George was smart, athletic, kind, everything I wanted to be when I grew up. Right then and there, Mrs. George went from being just my teacher to becoming my ultimate role model.

I had a broken arm, but I was still grounded. So the rest of the week and most of the weekend was spent working on my project. The excitement of coming up with my idea had contributed to me breaking my arm, but at least I wasn't banging my head anymore. Everyone loved my idea and my famous person was perfect for me.

I was going to be a player of the All-American Girls Professional Baseball League. This baseball league broke barriers for women in sports. Women were finally given a chance to play, and to earn the respect to play sports professionally, just like men.

It was perfect. I had plenty of time on my hands now with my broken arm and no sports for six weeks, so my wax museum project was my first and only priority.

The day of the wax museum was monumental. Our school was full of parents, grandparents, aunts, uncles, and more. I had an amazing backdrop of an old time stadium that I painted on a large white cloth canvas. The backdrop had a large grandstand seating area and vines growing on the outfield wall. I wore a replica woman's baseball outfit that was sewn by my grandmother. I had practiced at least a million times and I was ready.

Game time baby!

Mrs. George walked up to me frozen in my place, looked me in the eyes, and snapped her fingers to bring me to life. Her clipboard rested across her forearm and she clicked her pen in preparation to grade me on my final project. I stood frozen in time. My body trembled with nerves and my voice had suddenly escaped my throat. Mrs. George tried

to revive my character with a second finger snap, and I knew it was now or never. The final seconds on the clock, the last inning, I had to take control and win the game. Confidence circulated through my body, and I began.

"Hello, I am a Rockford Peach and I am a member of the All-American Girl Professional Baseball League. In 1943, my husband was drafted to serve our country in World War II, and the first all-woman professional baseball league was born.

I traveled from city to city with my teammates reviving baseball in our country and keeping Americans entertained, while the men of our country fought in the war. The All-American Girls Professional Baseball League gave over six hundred women a chance to play professional baseball. The League ran from 1943 to 1954.

I am also in the Baseball Hall of Fame in Cooperstown, New York. I am an important part of American History because I broke a barrier proving that girls can do everything a boy can do."

As I froze back into place, Mrs. George turned her clipboard to show me my grade. I did a double take! Right by my name she had written A+! I broke from my frozen stance to celebrate with my victory dance.

> Drumroll to the left
> Drumroll to the right
> Fist pump and a jump—Yes!
> Fist pump and a jump—Yes!
> Fist pump and a jump—Yes!

By the end of the wax museum project, I knew that everyone, including Mrs. George, believed what I believed. Girls can play sports, too.

CHAPTER 7

Six weeks had finally passed and I was crawling out of my skin to get this cast off and get back on the field. The doctor said I was good to go—just in time to play my last game with my soccer teams before the spring soccer seasons came to an end.

Luckily, when one sport ends, another begins. It was time for baseball and softball. Just like soccer, I play on a boys' baseball team and a girls' softball team. Despite having to take such a long break, pre-season practices went smoothly—I was still fast and could make it to home plate before the outfielder had even touched the ball. Our fields did not have outfield fences, so my batting strategy was to power the ball over an outfielder's head and run. Too bad Dad and I didn't have a deal of the day for my baseball and softball games, I would have had a lot of great meals from all of my home runs.

I love playing sports. It's what I do. I'm good at it and that's my jam. But I also love watching sports—especially with my big brother Owen. We play catch sometimes, and we watch sports, he is the one person who I never have to explain my love of sports to. He just gets it. He loves sports too. He gets me.

One Sunday morning, Owen and I got caught up watching professional wrestling before my baseball game. Professional wrestling is very entertaining and losing track of time is pretty easy when there is a cage match involved. While we watched, Owen and I imitated their actions and did fancy wrestling moves of our own. Owen is much bigger than I am, so he holds the championship belt in our house and he is determined to make sure it stays that way. While

Owen had me in a lock down hold, I was doing everything in my power to reverse the direction of the match when Mom and Dad came home from a quick trip to the grocery store. They hollered for me to meet them in the car. Even though my parents told me before they left that I needed to be ready in 30 minutes, I had completely forgotten to get ready for my baseball game.

Responsibility was an important lesson at my house. I knew that already, but it was reinforced often—and it was about to be reinforced again. "Lily, it is your job to get your equipment packed and your uniform on. The team is counting on you to be there on time, and Dad and I have a lot of running around we have to do today," Mom said annoyed.

It was time to go and I wasn't even close to ready. Crazily, I ran around the house, throwing my uniform on and grabbing my bat bag. On the ride to my baseball game I realized I had forgotten something really important. I didn't have my hat.

Yes, I could play without my hat, but my hat was my disguise when I was playing on the boys team. I could wrap my hair up in a perfect bun, since I played way out in the outfield, and no boy on the other team would suspect that I was a girl.

When I was little, it didn't matter as much, but now that I was getting older, I was more self-conscious about the other team finding out that I was a girl. I begged Mom and Dad to turn the minivan around, but they were all about teaching me wonderful life lessons like responsibility, blah, blah, blah, and they continued driving to the ballpark.

Dad said, "If we go back to get your hat now, we'll miss the first few innings of the game. That's not what a good team player does, Lily."

Mom added, "And that will just stress everyone out anyway. That's not good to do on a game day." Mom and Dad were right again. We had no time to go back home.

We arrived at the ballpark on time, with my uniform tucked in neatly, my eye black painted just above my cheeks, and my long blonde ponytail swaying in the wind.

I played first base to start the game and of course, had to be right next to the opposing team's dugout. They spotted me right away and the whispers and taunting began.

"Where is your dress, first base?"

"They have a girl, we will crush this team for sure!"

I focused on the game this time—no more letting them get to me—and I put those nasty comments out of my mind. I have to admit I was glad when we switched positions after the third inning and I was away from their team, but I was proud that I didn't let it affect me. I was quicker than most of them anyway, and once they saw that, there were no more comments.

The game was what my parents call a "barnburner" because it was really exciting and close. I've never really understood what that has to do with burning a barn, but I hear enough parents and grandparents saying it that it must be an exciting thing to see.

We were the home team and it was the final inning of the game. The score was tied 1-1 and I was up to bat. I have to admit those nasty boys may have gotten to me a little, at least on offense, because I was hitless thus far in the game. As I walked up to the plate I could hear our fans chanting my name.

"Lily! Lily! Lily!"

I had never been so focused. I twisted my hands around the bat and gritted my teeth. I replayed the mean comments the other team had said in my mind, which fueled my fire and intensity even more. As the pitcher released the ball it looked like a huge beach ball floating my way. I swung and smoked a line drive right up the middle and back at the pitcher's face. The pitcher dodged and ducked to save his face from being smashed by the ball. He lost his balance, tripped, and landed right on his butt. I sprinted down the first baseline and was safe with a single. I flashed a smirk of a smile toward the opposing team's dugout and flipped my ponytail that stuck out from the bottom of my helmet. I had never been so proud to be a sporty girl.

I advanced to second on a perfectly executed sacrifice bunt by Malik. With one out, my best bud, Carter, was up to bat. Carter was a great hitter and he was due. Carter swung at the first pitch and hit a liner in the right field gap. I was on my horse running toward third. My coach was jumping and waving me to go all the way home.

I pushed off the inside corner of third base with home plate just 60 feet away. I looked up and saw that the catcher had his glove out preparing to catch the ball from the relay man. I gave it everything I had and pushed my body toward home. I dove head first touching home plate before the catcher could tag me out.

I was safe! We had won the game! I did my victory dance and the rest of the team gathered in a huddle and joined me in the dance they had seen me do a million times:

>Drumroll to the left
>
>Drumroll to the right
>
>Fist pump and a jump—Yes!
>
>Fist pump and a jump—Yes!
>
>Fist pump and a jump—Yes!

After our celebration, it was time to shake the other team's hands. I stood in line with my team, began to walk across the field, and stuck my hand out to wish the other team a "good game." As I walked by, every single player on the opposing team intentionally pulled their hand away so they didn't have to touch mine. With each player that I passed my confidence sunk lower and lower into the dirt infield. I knew it was time for a change and my days of playing with the boys might be over.

On the car ride home, everyone seemed to have forgotten my irresponsibility and the hat fiasco before the game, which was good, but I couldn't get it out of my mind. Forgetting my hat was the reason that my identity was revealed and the reason I was treated differently.

"Maybe everyone is right and girls aren't supposed to play sports," I whispered to myself. I daydreamed the rest of the car ride imagining my life without sports. Being a lady, sipping tea, and making crafts was not my idea of daydreaming. It was a nightmare.

CHAPTER

Thankfully, my nightmare of sipping tea and being proper was short-lived, because later that night Mom and Dad shared the best news ever with me.

"Lily, I saw how the boys on the other team reacted when you scored the winning run today. I'm sure that made you feel pretty sad. Would you be interested in playing with girls that love sports as much as you do?"

"Yes! That would be awesome! Are there other girls out there as competitive as me?" I asked.

"You bet Lily! There are select teams you can try out for. The word "select" means you could be chosen to be on the team if you do well at the tryouts," Dad explained.

I already knew what a select team meant because Owen plays select basketball. But I had no idea they offered select sports for girls, too. A select softball team would allow me to play with just girls—girls that loved sports as much as I do. There would be no more need to hide my identity. I could be proud of being a sporty girl.

Dad said, "Great, Lily, we'll get you signed up for tryouts first thing in the morning."

I couldn't wait. I spent the rest of the night planning my practice schedule and envisioning myself making the team.

Tryouts were in a week and I knew that I would need to prepare. I wanted to make the team so badly that nothing could get in my way. Owen and the neighborhood boys helped me practice a lot of baseball skills to get me ready for my tryout, and Dad and I played catch almost every night. We worked on pop flies, grounders, pitching, and hitting. Tryouts were coming quickly and I was pumped up!

A few days later, Dad dropped me off at the tryout and wished me luck. I shut the car door, looked back and said, "I don't need any luck because I have skill."

Walking to the field with my bat bag hanging on my back and my head held high, I began sizing up my competition. One girl caught my eye. She looked like she could be trying out for a high school team, not a ten and under team. She was tall and had a big bump on each arm. These bumps were not mosquito bites or even goose bumps because it was a chilly day. These two bumps were muscles and I was officially nervous. I heard one of her friends call her Dinah. Never heard that name before!

There were about twenty girls at the tryout and I quickly did the math in my head. Only nine girls play on the field at once and they would need a few players on the bench. At a maximum they would take thirteen players, so that meant out of the twenty girls at the tryout, seven of us wouldn't make the team. I didn't recognize any of these girls. There wasn't one girl from my elementary school and very quickly I felt like a little fish in a very big pond.

I hung up my bat bag and pulled out my glove. A girl about a head taller than me said "Hi, I'm Haylee. What's your name?"

"I'm Lily. Want to play catch?"

"Sure!" and she grabbed a ball from the bucket and headed to left field.

Together we played catch and it eased my nerves to loosen up my arm and chat with a new friend. Turns out Haylee is a grade ahead of me, which explains why she is so tall. We have a lot in common. This is her first tryout with an all-girls team, too, and she used to play on an all-boys team, too.

After talking with Haylee, I hoped we would both make the team because she would be a great friend.

Soon after playing catch, the tryouts began. First, the coaches tested our outfield arm strength.

I was able to throw the ball pretty well, but the coaches kept telling me to throw the ball on a line and not like a rainbow. I had never heard those terms before, as no one has ever instructed my throwing. I always had the strongest arm. I quickly figured out from observing the other girls that "on a line" meant hard, fast, and straight like a bullet.

Following outfield drills we worked on grounders in the infield. I stood at the back of the line feeling a little intimidated. When it was my turn to field the grounder, the coach accidently lifted his grounder into the air. I flipped my glove over beautifully to catch the line drive. The ball was coming towards my glove and I made the mistake of taking my eye off of it.

Rule #1 in softball: Never take your eye off the ball.

The ball nicked the top of my glove, spun off right into my lip, and dropped to the dirt.

My lip stung, it bled, but I had to be tough. I wiped the small amount of blood, from my lip and asked the coach for another grounder. Coaches love kids who show enthusiasm and the desire to be better. The next ball I fielded cleanly and hustled to the back of the line. I made it through grounders with three fielded balls and one bloody error.

Finally, we had an opportunity to hit and scrimmage. I tapped the bat on my cleats to clear off the dirt just like the pros. My feet were shoulder length apart with a slight bend in the knees, my bat was perched just off my left shoulder, just like my favorite KC Royals hitters did. My batting stance was athletic and my eyes were on the ball in the pitcher's glove. I took the first pitch because it was a ball—high and outside. The second pitch landed right in my hitting zone. I pounded a zinger to second base and sprinted down the line. Haylee, my new friend, was playing second base. She took three steps to the right and in one miraculous movement, she dove to scoop up my hit, and from her knees threw me out at first base just in time.

The defensive players on Haylee's team ran to give her a quick high five and then ran back to their positions. I was happy for Haylee's amazing play, but bummed that I didn't get on base.

Later in the scrimmage, Dinah, the arm-bumps-girl, walked up to the plate. She scared the living daylights out of me. She was like the girl version of the Incredible Hulk. She pounded on the plate, demanding a strike, and smacked the first pitch into the right field gap. I was gawking, watching her run as she rounded first base. I was playing second base, and should have been running out to get the relay, but instead I was frozen in the baseline and right in her way. She was a runaway freight train charging at me and I was a statue back in the wax museum and couldn't move. The train didn't stop and plowed right through me.

"Get out of the way, girl!" she yelled as I fell butt-first onto the dirt. The Hulk pumped her fists and zipped around second, third, and finally slid into the plate for a homerun. She

didn't even need to slide, because the outfielders were still chasing her blast of a hit way out where the fence should have been. I watched in amazement from my view in the dirt. Dinah was Dinah-mite.

I left the tryout knowing I gave my best effort, but feeling that I was way out of my league. I wasn't confident that I was one of the top thirteen players at the tryout. I needed instruction in the outfield on my throwing, I got smacked in the face during grounders, I didn't get a hit in the scrimmage, and the Hulk knocked me on my butt to end my tryout. Maybe I could have used some of that luck dad offered before tryouts. So much for thinking I was the only sporty girl in the world. It was a good feeling knowing other girls liked sports as much as I did. This was definitely the challenge I have been waiting for.

Following the tryout, the coaches got together and discussed their observations and evaluations of the players. Then they created the team and made phone calls letting the players know if they were selected or not. I was restless and barely touched Mom's tuna and noodle casserole. I couldn't sit at the table eating more yellow food. It's impressive that one human being can create that many fairly good-tasting yellow food combinations.

I paced with the cordless phone in my hand waiting for it to ring. After nearly four hours, it finally rang and it wasn't my grandma or a telemarketer. It was the coach of the Nebraska Flight Select Softball Team. I threw the phone at my dad and made him do the talking. I was too nervous and needed assistance for this call.

My dad smiled and took the phone from me. I could only hear my dad say, "Yes. Yes. Yes. Uh huh. I understand." He chatted with the coach for a few minutes while writing down notes on piece of paper. In my mind I was thinking, *Yes!* The notes on the paper had to be about where we would play our games… or what number they gave me for my jersey…or what states we would be traveling to.

Dad smiled, but wouldn't make eye contact as he thanked the coach for the call. He hung up the phone and placed it on the end table in slow motion even though my mind was in fast forward.

"Lily, let's talk," Dad said.

Usually when someone says "Let's talk," it's bad news. But this couldn't be! I bounced over to my dad and plopped on his lap with a huge grin.

"Tell me the scoop! What position am I going to play? When do we start practices? What number am I? Where am I in the batting order? Tell me! Tell me! Tell me!"

He placed his arm around my shoulders and started speaking in his calm and gentle voice. Where was his, *you did it* excited scream? Why wasn't he lifting me in the air and twirling me around?

"Lily, you didn't make the team. The coaches were very impressed by your talent, but they think you need another year under your belt to sharpen your skills. But the good news is, they would love to have you try out again next year."

Sharpen my skills? Why don't they just tell me I am a head shorter, a year younger, and just plain not as good as I need to be?

I looked up to fight back those dang tears. My eyes welled up and I tried not to blink, but it was like a kink in a garden hose had just come undone and a rush of water burst out. I blinked. The tears squirted out and I cried like a baby in my Daddy's arms.

CHAPTER 9

Summer arrived and not a day went by that I didn't think about the tryout. I was more motivated and determined than ever. I practiced all of my sports every day and there was no doubt that my skills would be the sharpest out there next year. I'll be a year older, now let's just hope I grow about four inches.

One June night while practicing softball with my dad, Mom hollered out the window that I had a phone call. I ran inside and grabbed the phone from mom.

"Hello." I said, wondering who would be calling me.

"How's it going, Lily?" I instantly recognized the voice on the other end. It was the Nebraska Flight's softball coach. My heart began to race as I listened to what he had to say. I couldn't believe my ears.

"Lily, two of the girls on the team are unable to travel to the state tournament. You were one of our alternates, and we'd like to know if you would want to play in their place this weekend?"

He had barely finished asking and I had already shouted, "Yes!"

I did my victory dance silently with one hand, while I was still on the phone getting the details from the coach, as mom and dad watched laughing.

Drumroll to the left

"Yes, I can be at practice tonight at 7:00 on the field." I smiled to Mom, put my hands together begging her silently to agree, and she nodded and mouthed "Yes."

Drumroll to the right

"Yes, my parents can drive me to the tournament Friday night." I looked at Dad and raised my eyebrows, grinning from ear to ear as I sort of asked him at the exact same time I was volunteering him. He smiled huge and mouthed "Yes."

Fist pump and a jump—Yes!

"I'll see you tonight!"

Fist pump and a jump—Yes!

"I'll make you proud!"

Fist pump and a jump—Yes!

"Thanks, Coach!"

CHAPTER 10

The second hand on the clock crawled at a snail's pace and the minutes seemed to be frozen. Tick. Tick. Tick. Time stood still and I thought I was going to die of excitement, fear, and anxiety. I played the game a million times in my mind... catching a high pop fly in the outfield or hitting a line drive up the middle, or scoring the winning run.

I heard the words I have been waiting for forever. "Lily, it's time to head out!"

It was game day, baby.

My cleats dug into the dirt, I smelled the freshly-mowed grass on the perfectly-manicured field, and I could feel my heart beating in my chest.

I took a moment to think about and appreciate the ladies of the Rockford Peaches paving the way for girls like me to play sports. Although frozen in history, they continued to move and motivate me.

"PLAY BALL!" It was like Mrs. George's snap during the wax museum, and suddenly I was awakened and ready to perform, along with my teammates.

My teammates. My teammates. That was music to my ears.

I played right field the first game, and even got a single down the third base line.

By the next morning, we had won three games in the tournament, and had made it to the championship game. We were just one game away from being state champions.

Our last game was against the Flights's biggest rival, the Dominators. I had played right field well all weekend and was glad that I was playing there again. I felt comfortable there for such a big game. Both pitchers were having fantastic games, and neither team had scored or even gotten past second base. In the bottom of the seventh inning, we were the home team and were up to bat. All we needed to do was score one run and we would win.

There were two outs and I was up to bat. I had never played in front of this many people before, and the stadium was filled to capacity. The fans were on their feet, cheering and chanting my name. "Lily! Lily! Lily!" I love that sound. It never gets old hearing people cheer my name.

I looked down at my knees and they were knocking with nerves. Suddenly I thought about Mrs. George's words "*Lily, the ball is in your court. Sports are for girls, too.*" I took a deep breath and stepped into the left side batter's box. The opposing pitcher had great control and threw very fast. I had never seen anything like her before.

The first pitch zoomed in as a strike right down the middle.

"Stee-rike one!" The umpire clenched his fist above his head and raised his pointer finger.

The Dominators's fans roared.

Through their cheers, I could still hear the chants of my name pushing me on. "Lily! Lily! Lily!"

I stepped out of the box and looked up at third base. The third basemen was playing really far back. Immediately I knew what I could do. The next pitch came in and I began to move my feet in the batter's box. The Dominators warned their players, "BUNT!"

I placed my bat flat and deadened the ball with my bat just like Owen had taught me. The ball spun in the dirt about five feet in front of home plate toward the third base line, staying fair. The third basemen sprinted towards the ball, fielded it, and threw a rocket toward first base. I buried my head and didn't look up until I touched first base just beating the first baseman's catch. I beat the throw by a step, and I was safe. The crowd went wild.

I looked at my coach for a signal, and he touched his arm and then his nose. *Game on!* He gave me the signal to steal. As soon as the pitcher released the next pitch to the batter, I took off and ran like the wind. I slid into second base and slid right under the tag.

Safe at second!

There I was on second base. I looked at my coach again for another signal. *Oh my gosh, was I reading the signal right?* He gave the steal sign again!

I led off, feeling like my feet had left the dirt and I was flying toward third.

I plunged toward the dirt head first and slid just as the catcher's throw soared over the third baseman's head.

I was safe.

The ball continued toward left field. I shot up from the dirt and looked up at my Nebraska Flight team. As I sprinted toward home plate and victory, my teammates were all jumping up and down and running out of the dugout to meet me as I landed firmly on home plate with both feet. The crowd went wild, my teammates hugged and high-fived, and my victory dance just took over from there.

Drumroll to the left
Drumroll to the right
Fist pump and a jump—Yes!
Fist pump and a jump—Yes!
Fist pump and a jump—Yes!
And then I added one more....
Fist pump and a jump—State Champs!

About the Author

Author Kelsey Maxell has been an elementary school teacher for more than a decade, and holds a Master's Degree in Elementary Education with a special emphasis in literacy. She and her husband, Ben, have two girls and live near Omaha, Nebraska. In her free time, she loves running, playing volleyball, softball, soccer, traveling and reading. Maxell is a former collegiate softball player and was a Division II National Champion in 2001.

Kelsey's mission in her writing is to create books that celebrate girls and encourages them to go for whatever they want! Her family stays active, and Maxell believes that any physical activity should be an important part of every girl's life, no matter what the activity or sport is.

Acknowledgments

Thank you to my students for your great ideas and enthusiasm. Your zest for learning inspires me to teach everyday.

Thanks Mom and Dad, for always believing in me—no matter what I'm doing.

Thank you to my husband, Ben, for your constant love and support.

Thank you to my friend Amanda George, for all your hard work on the illustrations, your humor and creativity, and for keeping me going every day.

Thank you to Lisa Pelto, Ellie, and Rachel of Concierge Marketing Inc. for seeing the purpose in my vision with this book series, and for making my dream of publishing a reality.

Made in the USA
Lexington, KY
18 February 2016